Original title:
Secrets of the Sequoia

Copyright © 2025 Creative Arts Management OÜ
All rights reserved.

Author: Lucas Harrington
ISBN HARDBACK: 978-1-80567-187-9
ISBN PAPERBACK: 978-1-80567-486-3

The Reminiscence of the Roots

In the forest, trees wear shoes,
Dancing roots with silly views.
They chuckle as they twist and twine,
And play hopscotch beneath the pine.

A squirrel once threw a grand ball,
With acorns stacked, they had a ball.
But one nut rolled, and chaos spread,
Now trees wear hats made from old led.

The gnarled roots tell tales at night,
Of raccoons dressed as knights in flight.
They laugh about that time last spring,
When twigs got caught in a bird's wing.

So if you wander near the grove,
Just listen close and you'll behold,
Those whispers of joy, oh what a sight,
In the land where the trees take flight.

Meditations Among the Giants

Beneath the giants, shadows play,
Where leaves gossip at the end of day.
A bear once wore a top hat, too,
He claimed he was the king, it's true!

The fungi dance, a ballet bright,
In polka dots and pure delight.
They spread the news of last night's feast,
With woodland creatures, joy increased.

Tall trunks are serious, but wise,
They poke their bark with playful sighs.
"Don't climb too high!" they gently croak,
"Or lose your hat in the wild smoke!"

So find a spot and watch the fun,
The creatures play beneath the sun.
These giants chuckle in the breeze,
Whispering tales among the trees.

Beneath the Needle-Laden Sky

Beneath the needle-laden sky,
The squirrels plot with a hasty sigh.
They'll steal those acorns, it's quite a feat,
While birds in laughter dance on their feet.

The pinecones gather round for a show,
As chipmunks juggle, oh what a pro!
The trees can't help but chuckle with grace,
As critters run wild in this lively space.

Tales from the Forest Floor

Down on the forest floor, what a sight,
The mushrooms gossip, not caring of light.
"Did you hear what the oak tree said?"
"Only if you'll share that pie, I'll tread!"

The beetles march in their shiny parade,
While ants form a caravan, never afraid.
With laughter they gather, fall into line,
Beneath whispering branches, they toast with sweet wine.

The Silent Watchers

The ancient giants stand tall and proud,
With bark as their cloak, they whisper aloud.
"Look at these creatures, they dance while we wait,"
"Let's drop a branch, it'll open the gate!"

The owls roll their eyes at the foolish display,
"Why do they prance when they could just sway?"
But the trees just chuckle, their laughter a breeze,
"Let them enjoy, it's their world to tease!"

Giants of Time and Earth

In a land where time takes a leisurely stroll,
The giants sip tea from a mossy old bowl.
With leaves piled high as their floral adorn,
They giggle at shadows that flicker and warn.

"Have you seen the rabbits in paint-splattered shoes?"
"They think they can hop, but they'll surely lose!"
The giggles radiate through the cool, shady air,
As these grand old trees sit in whimsical flair.

Beneath the Branches' Veil

In the shade where squirrels play,
Chipmunks chat about their day.
Whispers float on breezy trails,
Tales of acorns, and tiny fails.

From the ground, the roots do laugh,
As the branches draft a path.
Bumblebees with gossip swirl,
In this tallwood, joy does twirl.

The Quiet Choir of Nature

A rustle here, a croak from there,
Frogs that sound like they don't care.
Leaves applaud the tiny beats,
As nature hums its kooky feats.

Singing trees wear leafy hats,
While raccoons throw food at cats.
In this harmony of fun,
Every critter shares a pun!

Sentinels of the Sunlight

Tall and proud, they stand in line,
Their bark is rough, but oh, they're fine!
With knots and grooves that tell a tale,
Of windy days and rains that pale.

But watch them laugh, as shadows dance,
Each photo feels like a comical chance.
Photobombers, clouds that drift,
The sunlight gives a merry lift.

Enigma Within the Rings

Count the rings, what do they say?
One fell over on laundry day!
Time's a jester, spinning threads,
In the grooves, where wisdom spreads.

They hide some giggles, tuck away,
Mysterious laughs, they could relay.
Every year brings a new delight,
In whirls of growth, they take to flight.

Mesmerized by the Majestic

In the woods, giants sway with glee,
Whispering tales to birds and bees.
Their bark's a canvas, full of cheer,
Grooves like laughter, echoing near.

Squirrels plot with acorn schemes,
While raccoons dance in moonlit dreams.
The trees roll their eyes, play the fool,
As nature's jesters break all the rules.

The Untold Stories of Shade

Underneath the leafy embrace,
Dancing shadows move with grace.
Each stump has a secret, a chuckle so wide,
As creatures peep and take a ride.

The rabbits gossip, the mice exchange winks,
While above, the wise old owl thinks.
What tales to tell of sunlight's tease,
And how squirrels hoard more than just cheese?

Imprints of the Seasons Past

Footprints left on earthy floors,
Whispers of what happened before.
A snowman's laugh, a summer slide,
Frozen giggles they cannot hide.

The wind carries echoes, soft and light,
Of children's laughter, pure delight.
While leaves share rumors of the time,
A frog croaked jokes in perfect rhyme.

Celestial Canopy Underfoot

Stars above chuckle and play,
As branches sway in the Milky Way.
Beneath our feet, the twigs all crack,
The forest floor gives no slack!

Frogs croak tunes that seem absurd,
While fireflies flash like dancing birds.
Each step we take is a new ballet,
In this forest stage where giggles sway.

Portraits Painted in Green

In the forest where leaves tickle,
Trees wear coats that make them giggle.
A squirrel in a bow tie dashes,
While rabbits practice their high-stakes clashes.

The branches twist in playful tricks,
Chasing shadows, they pull great kicks.
A toadstool ballet beneath the boughs,
Leaves applaud with their rustling vows.

Aligning with the Ancient Spirits

The spirits whisper in a tree's deep bark,
While chipmunks chuckle, giving spark.
   Old pine needles toss fuzzy jokes,
    As owls blink and play the folks.

  They dance in rings with mossy ties,
   Sharing tales of their wise old lies.
  A raccoon winks, 'It's all in the fun!'
While nature giggles, 'We've just begun!'

The Legacy of Sylvan Giants

The giants flex, reach for the sun,
Making shadows where laughter has fun.
With roots so twisted, they trip and fall,
In this grand quest, they're the clowns of all.

A sapling whispers, 'What's the deal?'
While bumblebees mix in with zeal.
Old woodpeckers pick out the best tunes,
As squirrels throw acorns like festive balloons.

Tribe of the Tall

In the tribe where the tallest reside,
All the birds take a swoop on the slide.
They share puns from branches so wide,
As wiggly leaves have nothing to hide.

With echoes of laughter, they sway and swing,
While ants bring snacks to this leafy fling.
A festival blooms under the moon's glow,
In this leafy realm, humor's the show!

In the Heart of the Ancient Grove

In a forest so tall, the trees whisper and chuckle,
Their trunks hold the tales of a squirrel's great struggle.
Raccoons plot pranks with a mischievous gleam,
While owls roll their eyes at the daylight's bright dream.

The crows croak of gossip and rumors galore,
A woodpecker's dance makes the branches implore.
With all of this laughter, the roots start to wiggle,
Each leaf trying hard not to snicker or giggle.

Veils of Moss and Memories

Beneath fluffy veils where the green shadows play,
The moss-covered logs have their own tales to say.
A snail race is gleeful, with laughter in tow,
While mushrooms host parties for bugs in a row.

Each droplet of dew is a wink and a nod,
As the frogs swap their jokes, giving all a good prod.
The sun peeks through branches, the leaves start to sway,
In this raucous old grove, it's a humorous day!

The Language of Leaves

Whispers abound in the fluttering green,
Leaves share the gossip, with tales yet unseen.
A breeze fuels the laughter, a rustle, a shout,
As branches shake hands and dance all about.

Two leaves sharing secrets, a twirl in the air,
A conifer giggles, throwing needles with flair.
Their chatter is joyful, a woodland delight,
As shadows are cast in the warm afternoon light.

Beyond the Roots

Down deep in the soil, the critters all scheme,
Earthworms tell tales of a wild, wiggly dream.
A badger, quite serious, dons glasses and ties,
While shrews pen their stories with clever replies.

The roots dance below, in a silent ballet,
Plotting their antics, in jest, come what may.
For beneath all the laughter, there's wisdom so grand,
In this jumble of life, all is well, hand in hand.

Growth Rings of Forgotten Legends

In the bark there are whispers, so wide,
Of knights and their horses, once filled with pride.
A squirrel in armor, a battle to fight,
But lost in the acorns, he fell out of sight.

Old roots tell of pranks, with a chuckle and cheer,
Of raccoons with crowns, and a party right here.
The owls throw confetti, the leaves start to sway,
While the branches all giggle at the end of the day.

A Tapestry of Time-Worn Tales

Each knot in the wood holds a tale of delight,
Of mischievous bugs having parties by night.
A worm with a top hat spins tales that entice,
While bees share a drink and pretend they're so nice.

The moss wears a grin and listens so well,
As frogs recite limericks within their small shell.
With a rustle and shuffle, the stories unfold,
Of misfits and jesters, in laughter behold.

The Stillness Between the Trees

In the hush of the woods, where the shadows play,
A giggling breeze makes the branches sway.
A fox tells a joke to the deer and the hare,
And the laughter erupts—like confetti in air!

A snail with a joke book, slow as can be,
Slips on by, while the chipmunks all glee.
In the stillness, they dance, and they twirl in delight,
Making shadows and sunshine as they play through the night.

Echoes of the Tumbling Streams

Where the river sings softly, with water so spry,
The fish are all gossiping, oh my, oh my!
With bubbles of laughter, they share their own puns,
And the kingfisher chuckles—who needs a cap gun?

A turtle in shades swims with style and with grace,
While otters are sliding all over the place.
With a ripple of joy and a splash in the sun,
The stream carries laughter—oh, what fun we've spun!

Whispers of the Forest Elders

Old trees gossip in the breeze,
Mossy beards float with such ease.
Squirrels break the sacred truce,
Laughing hard as they hoot and juice.

Roots intertwine like tales long spun,
Beneath the sun, they dance and run.
A woodpecker's drum is quite the beat,
But watch your step, don't lose your feet!

The Lullaby of Longing Limbs

Stretching high to catch some rays,
Branches sigh in drowsy ways.
A playful breeze gives them a shove,
For there's no limb that lacks some love.

Whispers tickle the tufts of green,
Nature's giggle is hardly seen.
Boughs sway and bend in comical style,
They share a wink that lasts a while.

Lurking in the Dappled Light

Shadows dance beneath the trees,
Raindrops giggle with every tease.
Frogs sing low beneath the fray,
While lizards hide, come out to play.

Barks reveal their knowing grins,
As critters plot their wild little sins.
But the sunlight's here, so bright and fierce,
Who knows what pranks these trees may pierce?

Nature's Hidden Chronicles

In every ring, a story dwells,
Of wise old mammals and their spells.
Roots like fingers point at fun,
Inviting us to join the run.

Bees buzz in a choir of hums,
While ants parade like tiny drums.
A giggle spins the night to dawn,
In forests where the fun goes on.

Echoes Beneath the Bark

In a forest so grand, there's whispers of cheer,
Trees cracking jokes, for everyone to hear.
"Why did the twig cross the path?" they would say,
"To branch out and find a new leaf for the day!"

With laughter that rustles through needles so high,
The squirrels all giggle as they scurry by.
"Don't be knotty," they bark, "just go with the flow,
We'll branch out together and let our roots grow!"

Guardians of the Green

There once was a tree with a floppy old hat,
He claimed he could dance, but he looked more like that.
The leaves rolled their eyes as the branches swayed,
"Careful with that move, you might just cascade!"

The mushrooms would chuckle at his silly stance,
"Just stick to the shade; don't risk a mischance!"
But the tree kept on grooving, with roots in the groove,
In the dance of the woods, he found his own move!

Dreams in the Redwood Realm

In the heart of the woods where the tall ones grow,
The fairies play pranks, putting on a real show.
"Last night we swapped nests with the wise old owls,
Now they think they're flamingos wearing pink towels!"

The deer stop to giggle at the sight so absurd,
As a hedgehog in boots hops along, quite disturbed.
"Have you seen my lost socks?" he questions each sprou

With laughter echoing, there's no room for doubt!

Mysteries of the Timbered Towers

Up high in the trees where the secrets keep clear,
A raccoon once wore a monocle, quite dear.
He'd hold fancy meetings, drinking dew from a cup,
"Who's got the best nuts? Vamos, let's sup!"

The crows rolled their eyes, with a caw and a flap,
"Raccoon's on a roll, someone get him a map!"
Yet the wise old tree just chuckled with glee,
"Let's toast to the heist—of the best, you all see!"

Ramblings of the Rooted Giants

In the forest a whisper grows,
Roots chat like gossipy crows.
Beneath the bark, they spill the tea,
About birds' antics and buzzing bees.

Each ring holds a story to share,
Of squirrels that dance without a care.
They laugh at storms that howl and rage,
While they stand firm like a forest sage.

The vines tease branches about their height,
Saying, 'Check out my sprouts, aren't they tight?'
Jokes exchanged through the swaying leaves,
Conspiring tales that one believes.

Oh, to be a tree with roots so deep,
Sharing the humor that nature keeps.
With every breeze, their laughter flies,
In the land where the tallest trees rise.

Shadows of Forgotten Days

Shadows twirl like dancers unseen,
In the mist, they frolic and preen.
Once they whispered of days so bright,
Now they giggle at trees taking flight.

Leaves rustle with secrets of yore,
Like children playing behind closed doors.
"Do you remember that acorn prank?"
They chuckle beneath the soft, cool bank.

Branches stretch, trying to flee,
From tales shared 'neath the old oak tree.
With every creak of an ancient limb,
A new joke born from shadows dim.

Oh hush, sweet shadows, stay awhile,
Let's spin our stories with a smile.
Here in the twilight, let laughter blend,
The past and present, forever friends.

Glimpses into the Green Abyss

Peeking through leaves, what do I spy?
A raccoon with dreams and an eye for pie.
Mossy creatures plot and conspire,
In the greenery, their laughter won't tire.

Ferns gossip about the old stone troll,
Who keeps a hoard that never grows small.
They snicker about his fuzzy old beard,
Saying it's the strangest they've ever heard.

A beetle blares tunes with gusto and grace,
While daisies twirl in a floral embrace.
With whispers of mischief, they paint the night,
Dancing shadows twirl under starry light.

Oh, what a world of giggles and cheer,
In that lush abyss, where sighs disappear.
Every glimpse brings forth a new giggle,
In the green, lets our laughter wiggle.

The Time Travelers of the Forest

Whispers of time weave through the trees,
Beneath the canopy, they nudge the breeze.
Time travelers, old and spry,
Sharing tales of how squirrels fly.

Branches stretch, reaching for the past,
Every nod of the head is a blast!
'You wouldn't believe what we used to do,'
Sang the saplings, a mischievous crew.

Twists of fate in the tangle of green,
A bear in a hat, oh what a scene!
They chuckle as they remember the days,
When moose wore boots in curious ways.

In the twilight, history has fun,
Branches wave like they've just begun.
Oh, to linger where tales drift and soar,
With time travelers, forever we explore.

The Language of Rings

In circles etched upon their barks,
Whispers of time play hide and seek.
With each new ring, a tale embarks,
Of squirrels that chatter and branches that creak.

A birthday cake with layers so grand,
Counting the years without a care.
Telling the tales of a clumsy hand,
That dropped a nut without a spare.

If trees could laugh, they'd roar and cheer,
At all the birds that missed their flight.
With giggles in wood, they'd lend an ear,
To tales of owls in the dead of night.

Camouflaged Clarity

In the shade of giants, shadows play,
A conga line of ants so spry.
They dance and parade in a woodland ballet,
Where even lost socks may try to fly.

The chattering chipmunks weave a plot,
To steal the acorns from right under.
But the tall trees, they know a lot,
And chuckle low, like distant thunder.

While the forest giggles, who's watching who?
You'd think it's all a masquerade!
Branches with eyes keep the chaos in view,
Playing tricks on the wood that they made.

Beneath the Skyward Spires

Beneath these towers, the wits collide,
Where a beetle boasts of battles won.
The punchlines grow like roots so wide,
In this comedy, all are having fun.

Rainbow hues lift up the gloom,
As butterflies giggle in flowered seams.
Busy bees buzz into the room,
With nectar tales and outlandish dreams.

Ticklish leaves overhead sway and tease,
While the clouds drift and toss up a pie.
In this circus beneath the trees,
Even the sun can't help but sigh.

A Tapestry of Time

The fabric of ages in fibers so thick,
Weaving laughter through every strand.
A snail's slow tale unfolds with a flick,
A stitch of joy as time takes its stand.

The raccoons giggle in midnight's glow,
Creating mischief with paws and paws.
While the wise old owls, in the tree's row,
Glean wisdom from blunders without a pause.

Each leaf a page in the book of the green,
Tales of mischief that would make you grin.
In the tapestry woven, a playful scene,
Where no frown is found and all glee begins.

The Essence in Every Leaf

In the canopy, leaves do sway,
Whispers giggle, come out and play.
Squirrels gossip, chips in tow,
Beneath the trees, all the fun flows.

Giant trunks with stories old,
Bark adorned in patches bold.
Nature's jesters, each branch grins,
As sunlight dances, joy begins.

Roots entangle, with a twist,
Tales of acorns we can't resist.
Who knew trees had such wild dreams?
Plotting mischief, it seems, it seems!

So come along, hear leaf-based laughs,
The forest's joy spills like warm puffs.
In this green world where giggles thrive,
Every leaf's laughter keeps us alive.

Secrets Above the Ground

High above where birds fly free,
Branches are buzzing, so much glee!
With knots and curves, they play a game,
Nature's own quirky, reclusive fame.

Mice peek out from their fluff-filled lair,
These woodland folks take life with flair.
Twisting vines, a playful race,
Who knew treetops held this much space?

A canvas of blooms in a tangled heap,
The pollen's tickle makes noses leap.
Laughing Larks serenade the day,
While other critters join the ballet.

All is fun where the squirrels prance,
Daring each other in a nutty dance.
In the canopy's playful surround,
Lies a joy that can astound!

The Stillness Between Whispers

Amidst large giants, a hush does fall,
Leaves share tales, but we know it all.
In the stillness, a rustle hints
At gossip brewing in nature's prints.

Beetles spin yarns in tiny tones,
Raccoons hold court on mossy thrones.
Together they craft a festival cheer,
Where the smallest sprites come to hear.

The shadows play tag with light's embrace,
A game of hide-and-seek, oh what grace!
Between the trunks, secrets collide,
In laughter we trust, nothing to hide.

So pause for a moment, let whispers flow,
Hear the merry tales and let laughter grow.
In this tranquil space, humor resides,
In a world where nature eternally guides.

Nature's Silent Chronicles

Under the watch of a wooden sage,
Time ticks slowly, page by page.
Each ring a story, a punchline sweet,
As critters plot their next happy feat.

In the dusk, shadows frolic, extend,
Nature's pals squeal, "Let's pretend!"
With twigs as wands, they craft their tales,
Adventures abound on feathered trails.

Bushy tails tell of acorn raids,
The bravest hearts in leafy parades.
As daydreams weave through roots so deep,
Count the giggles, and don't you sleep!

So gather round for a laugh or two,
Nature's chronicle in every hue.
Where every creature and tree unite,
To share the joy from day to night.

Time's Embrace in the Elderwood

In the woods where tall tales grow,
Trees gossip soft, secrets they know.
Old branches twist in a playful dare,
Whispers of squirrels float through the air.

Mossy hats on the tiny gnomes,
They laugh at their big, fallen homes.
With every breeze, a riddle's spun,
In the shade where the laughter's begun.

Acorns drop with a plop and a cheer,
For the forest, it's a seasonal affair.
Rabbits dance on a log so wide,
In Time's embrace, they take it in stride.

Underneath the quiet, russet crown,
The trees wear wisdom like a silly gown.
As twilight falls, the giggles appear,
Making memories that linger here.

Crickets and Canopies

Crickets chirp like they're on a stage,
With each high note, they turn the page.
A canopy casts where mischief hides,
In shadowy realms where laughter abides.

The tall trunks sway, they dance in a trance,
Leaves rustle softly, a natural dance.
A woodpecker knocks, he's seeking a tune,
As he drills for dinner, the sun starts to swoon.

Twinkling stars peek from boughs so wide,
Starlit folly, where joys collide.
The forest teems with giggles and plays,
Making memories in whimsical ways.

A raccoon winks, it's a cheeky affair,
As tree roots tickle without a care.
In this vibrant realm, both wild and free,
Lies a canvas of fun, just wait and see.

Threads of Verdant History

Among the knotted trunks, stories unfold,
Of mischief and magic, if one dares to hold.
Beneath the bark, a world so spry,
Where the owls tell tales of what's gone by.

Squirrels debate over acorn sizes,
While wise old tortoises share their prizes.
With giggles and chuckles, the fables ensue,
In a patchwork of laughter, there's always a clue.

The breeze carries whispers of age-old spree,
As ferns shimmy gently, wild and free.
Long ago, the Ponderosa sighed,
Cascading laughter where shadows bide.

Under the gaze of the moonlit sprite,
The forest bustles with joy each night.
With every step on the forest floor,
The threads of joy weave forevermore.

Beneath the Ancient Wisdom

Beneath the branches of the ancient wise,
Lies a treasure trove, a sweet surprise.
With giggling roots and paths well-tread,
The trees know the tales that make us red.

A squirrel with shades on takes a sunbath,
While chipmunks plot the next rascally path.
In this enchanted nook, they revel and roam,
Creating the quirkiest forest home.

The elder trees sway, with wisdom to lend,
Smiles stretching wide, like branches they bend.
In their company, days melt like ice,
Every moment wrapped in laughter, a paradise.

Frogs croak the tunes of whimsical lore,
While the wind rustles softly, begging for more.
Underneath the ancient, the stories are spun,
A funny little kingdom, where life's just begun.

Echoes of Elders in the Breeze.

In the woodland where giants sway,
   Leaves giggle in their leafy play.
Branches stretch with tales to share,
   Whispers float in the fragrant air.

Old trees gossip, with bark so thick,
   Telling tales of a squirrel's trick.
With acorn caps and wedged-in bread,
They chuckle loud, aged humor spread.

Mossy hats on knobby knees,
   All the wise ones bend with ease.
Crickets chirp a comical tune,
While shadows dance beneath a moon.

So if you stroll where woodlands meet,
   Listen close, those tales are sweet.
For nature's laughter fills the glade,
   As ancient trees play their charade.

Whispers in the Canopy

High above where the branches twist,
The leaves conspire, can't resist.
Squirrels plot with comedic flair,
While the woodpecker snickers in mid-air.

Every breeze brings a playful jest,
Tickling trunks where they might rest.
Cracking jokes in the sunny beam,
While beams of light create a dream.

Frogs will hop and sing their song,
Ribbiting rhythms, all day long.
Each old trunk has a laugh to lend,
And with each hug, the fun won't end.

So climb the branches, find their voice,
In the canopy, rejoice, rejoice!
For every whisper brings a smile,
A funny twist in nature's style.

Timekeeper's Embrace

Each ring inside a giant's core,
Holds memories—oh, what a store!
With every year and every laugh,
They mark the passage, nature's craft.

Tick-tock goes the woodpecker's beat,
As the old trunk rocks to a rhythm sweet.
While time bids fair to slow the day,
Beneath the shade, we leap and play.

With each tick, a giggle grows,
As flowers bloom and the summer glows.
Roots entwined with stories deep,
In their embrace, the laughter leaps.

So dance along with the game's delight,
In every shadow, there shines a light.
For time and laughter blend so well,
In the arms of trees, where tales dwell.

Shadows of the Ancient Giants

In the twilight where giants stand,
Shadows stretch across the land.
Their bark is old, but humor's young,
With stories sung and laughter flung.

Raccoons roam, jesters of the night,
While owls hoot with all their might.
Each whisper borne on the moonlit breeze,
Launches chortles through the trees.

Swinging vines like giggling friends,
Twisted branches, where the fun never ends.
Nature's jesters make no mistake,
In the forest, there's joy to partake.

So listen close as the night unfolds,
In the ancient shade, bright stories told.
With every rustle, a chuckle grows,
Among the mighty, where laughter flows.

The Enchantment of Old Growth

In the shadow of giants, they silently giggle,
Smoky jokes at the roots make the branches wiggle.
Whispers of time, with a twinkling eye,
As squirrels wear top hats and birds learn to fly.

Beneath the bark, there's a party of ants,
They shimmy and shake, in their tiny pants.
While trees play charades, their leaves all a-twirl,
Nature's own stage where the wild things whirl.

The mushrooms wear capes and the toads tap dance,
Encouraging laughter with every chance.
A forest of chatter, where gnomes brew cheer,
Old growth is silly, it's perfectly clear.

They crack up the moon with their ancient tales,
Mysteries float like soft autumn sails.
With each hearty laugh, the roots seem to grow,
In the land of the tall ones, fun surely flows.

Conversations with the Wind

The wind tells jokes as it breezes on by,
Tickling the leaves, making branches sigh.
It whispers tales of mischievous sprites,
Who borrow the sunshine to play all night.

"Did you hear?" says a gust, "it's true, I can fly!"
"Sure!" says a tree, dressed up to the sky.
With laughter and breezes, they tease all around,
Nature's loud whispers that bounce off the ground.

Breezy confessions bounce high in the air,
While petals and pollen spin without care.
Dancers in clouds twirling hieroglyphs bright,
Conversations with wind always end in delight.

So, listen intently when a breeze draws near,
You might hear a chuckle or catch a quick sneer.
The skies are alive with a humorous whim,
Each gust's a comedian; each laugh's a sweet hymn.

Serpents of Sunlight

Slithering rays play tag on the ground,
Wiggling through branches, making light sound.
The snakes of sun giggle as they weave,
Chasing their tails in the light of eves.

"Catch me if you can!" they shimmer and tease,
Dancing on leaves like a flamboyant breeze.
With sparkles to dazzle, they twist and they turn,
In a world full of giggles, there's so much to learn.

Beneath the big trees, the shadows have fun,
Playing hide and seek while the daylight runs.
Every whispering beam has a story to tell,
In the jocular forest where laughter's the spell.

So follow those rays, let your spirit take flight,
With serpents of sunlight leading you right.
Join in the frolic, don't miss out on the spree,
For sunshine's a joker in the grand canopy.

Unfurling the Unknown

Mysteries wrapped like an old gift's bow,
What lies in the shadows? We're eager to know!
A curl of the fern might bring giggles and glee,
As it dances and sways, wishing to be free.

The mushrooms are plotting, they're up to some tricks,
With spores full of giggles and riddles they mix.
They sap the tall trunks with their playful delight,
Chasing the moon till it's time for goodnight.

Each petal unfolds with a whimsical flair,
Revealing the funny in nature's great care.
The forest is hiding ridiculous charms,
With laughter and wonder, it happily warms.

So gather the stories that whisper and sing,
In the realm of the unknown, let your heart take wing.
Embrace the oddities you find as you roam,
For the forest's a jester, inviting you home.

Breath of the Subtle Giants

In a forest where giants stand tall,
Squirrels plot their acorn heist, after all.
Whispering leaves, they gossip and cheer,
While raccoons steal snacks, oh dear, oh dear!

Beneath a branch, a turtle sighs,
Laughing at birds as they practice their lies.
All the while, the clouds look down,
Wondering if they should wear a frown.

Mice tell tales of the trees' deep roots,
While owls hoot in polka-dotted boots.
Giant shadows stretch and sway,
Posing awkwardly like they want to play.

In the company of branches so wide,
Funny friendships bloom, side by side.
Who knew a forest could harbor such jest?
With laughter beneath their leafy vest.

Symphony of the Silent Grove

In the grove where silence reigns supreme,
A symphony plays, or so it would seem.
Crickets chirp out of tune, what a laugh!
While trees sway along, quite the gaff!

Beetles with brass, they strut and parade,
Each one convinced they're the next big grade.
The owls roll their eyes, quite unimpressed,
As the caterpillars form a music fest.

Branches wiggle to the sound of a breeze,
A happening place for woodland tease.
Even the mushrooms tap their shy toes,
In this concert of whimsy, anything goes!

When the sun sets, the stars begin to sway,
Echoing laughter through night and day.
For under the stars, the fun knows no bounds,
As nature giggles and joy resounds.

The Dance of the Evergreen Shadows

In shadows where evergreen smiles reside,
Trees spin around, their branches open wide.
A lively dance party in the shade,
With critters joining in, unafraid!

The hesitant fox takes center stage,
With two left paws, it's quite the rage.
While chipmunks cheer with a cartwheel or two,
Claiming they'll outdance the branches, who knew?

A wind gust blows, swaying them near,
As the shadows crack up while laughing with cheer.
In this secret bash, all frolic and prance,
Even the bumblebees join in the dance!

The ground shakes with joy, what a sight,
When shadows twist and spin with delight.
For in the heart of the trees, fun does not lack,
As laughter echoes and never looks back.

Sanctuary of Gracious Giants

In a sanctuary where kind giants lurk,
They share their wisdom with plenty of smirk.
Beneath the branches, the forest convenes,
Where raccoons plot and the pinecone queens.

A deer tells tales of the tallest trees,
While squirrels sketch plans like they're degrees.
Moss carpets the floor, a comfy throne,
As everyone gathers to share their own.

Intricate dances of the shadows at play,
With echoes of laughter from night into day.
As leaves shake their heads at the clumsy hare,
It tumbles and rolls without a care.

In the heart of this land, where joy multiplies,
Gracious giants laugh under wide-open skies.
For fun is a treasure they gladly provide,
In their sanctuary, where all can reside.

Whispers in the Grove

In the forest where the tall trees sway,
The squirrels gossip by the bright sunray.
They chuckle at the bark's big old grin,
While the rabbits joke about the raccoon's kin.

Leaves rustle as the story unfolds,
Of a woodpecker's tales that never gets old.
Mossy stones nod in laughter, they say,
This woodland life is a grand cabaret!

A chipmunk struts, dressed in his best plaid,
While a wise old owl ruffles feathers so mad.
"Who's the funniest?" they all want to know,
It's the playful deer, with their prancing show!

Beneath the laughter, strong roots intertwine,
In this amusing grove, everything's fine.
Come join the fun, it's a curious site,
Where every day feels like pure delight!

The Silent Sentinels

Tall guardians wear their rings of age,
Yet they giggle like kids on a playful stage.
With bark like armor, they root and stand,
Their laughter floats across the land.

In the shadows, small critters convene,
A squirrel shares jokes that are quite obscene.
The wise old branches just shake and sway,
No secrets here, just a bright ballet!

Listen close, and you might just hear,
The whispers of laughter - they're quite sincere.
Twisting vines tease in a friendly way,
Making mischief from night until day!

When breezes tickle the leaves so lush,
Every tree joins in a big, hearty hush.
But laughter rises, it's hard to contain,
Underneath the strong arms, joy will reign!

Beneath the Canopy

Beneath the branches where shadows dance,
The critters engage in a wild romance.
Starlight winks through the leaves so green,
A party of whimsy, oh what a scene!

The fireflies buzz with their tipsy glow,
While a wise raccoon puts on a show.
He juggles acorns, and the crowd goes wild,
Even the fawns can't help but be beguiled!

An old turtle slips, it's a comical sight,
As he rolls over, hoping to take flight.
Laughter erupts, leaves tumble and sway,
In this forest's heart, we play all day!

So join us here in this joyous spree,
Beneath the canopy, wild and free.
Friends intertwine, making merriment last,
In this whimsical world, time flies fast!

Echoes of Ancient Roots

Deep down in the soil where secrets keep,
Roots chuckle together, in whispers they leap.
They tell of old tales in a cheeky way,
Of a fox with a hat and a dog that could sway!

Mushrooms giggle with their funky hats,
While worms do the cha-cha, oh how they dance!
The sunbeams flicker, a disco delight,
Underneath the earth, it's a Saturday night!

Even the stones join the rhythm and beat,
Climbing up for a view, oh how sweet!
With ancient echo of laughter and glee,
Roots hold the stories of life's jubilee!

So peek underground, despite dirty looks,
This party's a laugh; it could fill books.
In the heart of the grove, let joy take its root,
Where fun is the fruit, oh ain't it a hoot!

Enigmas Among the Leaves

In the forest, trees tell tales,
Whispers float on breezy gales.
A squirrel dressed in party gear,
Claims to know all—never fear!

Toadstools tease with winks and grins,
They giggle as they spin their pins.
Hey, did you hear that branch's joke?
A leaf chuckled, 'I must be broke!'

A wise old owl sleeps on a throne,
Dreaming of acorns all alone.
But when he wakes and rubs his eyes,
He'll start a ruckus, what a surprise!

Underneath, the roots hold sway,
Chattering gossip day by day.
Just listen close, they're bound to share,
A tree with secrets? Oh, I swear!

The Heartbeat of the Woods

In the twilight, shadows dance,
Trees sway lightly in a trance.
A raccoon in a cape doth prance,
Declaring he's the woodland's lance!

Branches wiggle, quite enthused,
Frogs croak softly, feeling used.
`Did you hear the latest quirk?`
As a beetle shimmies, `What a perk!`

Tickling vines and sneaky twigs,
Play hopscotch 'round the dancing jigs.
A pinecone adds some flair and fun,
Claiming he's the only one!

The wind plays tricks, a playful tease,
As laughter ripples through the trees.
In this grove, joy's the best of goods,
Just ask the wise old neighborhood!

Reveries in the Arboreal

Beneath the boughs, where giggles creep,
   Napping saplings, dreams so deep.
  A chipmunk wears a tiny hat,
    Sipping tea, oh what of that?

Gnarled roots gossip with the breeze,
   They spread tales of hidden keys.
   `Did the owl just take a snooze?`
While mouldy acorns shout the blues!

Up high, where branches sway and bend,
   The laughter echoes with no end.
 A bird in shades flaunts fancy feathers,
  Spreading joy like sunny weathers!

Swaying leaves in a choreographed play,
 Pigeons strut on a leaf-strewn runway.
   What fun it is to swing and glide,
   In this wondrous, whimsical ride!

Threads of History in the Foliage

In the woods, where shadows loom,
Tales are stitched with laughter's loom.
A wild hare in a waistcoat stands,
Reciting tales of ancient lands!

Lichen whispers to mossy stones,
While ants march in fashion, oh what tones!
Each twig has stories, each leaf a plot,
Ever so clever, give it a shot!

Nutty squirrels toss acorns high,
Joining in on history's sly.
`Did you see that tree attempt a flip?`
Watch out, or you might take a trip!

So come, dear friend, enjoy the show,
Where every echo seems to glow.
In this realm of laughter and cheer,
Nature's whimsy draws us near!

Hidden Stories in the Bark

A tree that's tall, it hides its tales,
Whispered laughs in wooden gales.
Each ring a giggle, each knot a jest,
Nature's humor put to the test.

Squirrels chuckle as they scamper fast,
Plotting pranks that'll forever last.
When the branches shake, don't be alarmed,
It's just a joke that they've charmed.

Mossy riddles, bark with a grin,
Tickling the wind with secrets within.
A tree that's lively with stories to share,
Ask the woodpecker, he's quite aware.

So join the laughter, come one, come all,
In this forest, we'll have a ball!
The taller the tree, the funnier the punch,
Nature's giggles in a grand old brunch.

Shadows of a Giant

In the shade of giants, mischief brews,
Little critters plotting, sharing news.
They dance and twirl beneath the leaves,
Chasing after sunlight as it weaves.

A wise old owl hoots a playful tune,
While rabbits throw a party beneath the moon.
With acorns as snacks, they cheer and clap,
Each shadow holds a laugh, a silly map.

The bark transforms with every whim,
As stories bounce like a vibrant drum.
What happens next? Just take a peek,
You might find humor on a cheeky streak.

Giant roots that twist and twirl,
Creating playgrounds for all to whirl.
So in the shadows, let's spark a joy,
Join the amusing, every girl and boy.

Mysteries of the Timbered Realm

In the timbered realm where tall trees sway,
Mysteries revolve in a playful way.
With branches curling like a clown's nose,
Each whispering leaf a riddle that grows.

Squirrels in capes, racing up high,
Pretend they're heroes ruling the sky.
Beneath the trunks, the ants do cheer,
Cheesecake thoughts put legs in gear.

The owls in spectacles are wise and witty,
While frogs croak tunes that are quite the ditty.
In this realm of wonder, come take a stroll,
Where every twist in bark holds a playful role.

So grab a friend, and wander near,
In this timbered place, let's spread the cheer.
For every giggle among the trees,
Unfolds the fun with the greatest ease.

The Guardians of Time

Old trees stand tall, like guardians bright,
They tick-tock softly, a whimsical sight.
With squirrels as watchmen, all dressed in fur,
Keeping time with a cheeky purr.

Their rings counting years, but no one's in haste,
They laugh as they grow, with each little taste.
In the shadow of giants, where time takes a nap,
Every creature joins in for a giggle, a clap.

Mice in their caves plot out schemes,
While raccoons giggle in moonlit dreams.
The timekeepers chuckle as seasons pass by,
Dancing around under a starlit sky.

So raise your glass to the trees so wise,
With humor that sparkles like stars in the skies.
For in their embrace, laughter finds place,
And time, oh sweet time, becomes a wild chase.

Remnants of Ancient Echoes

Whispers of giants in the breeze,
Tickle the leaves, make them tease.
Who knew wisdom could be so tall,
With bark to laugh and branches that brawl?

Mighty trunks with humor to spare,
Tell tales of squirrels with fluffy hair.
They boast of acorns, grandest of feasts,
While jays just laugh at their tasty beasts.

Rooted in soil where laughter began,
These titans still jest, oh yes they can!
A tickling wind makes them sway side to side,
Shouting to streams, 'Come on, let's glide!'

In the forest, a comedy show,
Under the canopies, where giggles glow.
Nature's jest, it never is meek,
Just sit and listen—oh, how they speak!

Dialogues with the Ancient Ones

Gather around for tales so bright,
From giants who witnessed day and night.
Their voices rumble, a chuckle so deep,
Like old friends gathering, secrets to keep.

They gossip of times when dinosaurs roamed,
Of little green critters who did more than comb.
'Watch your step!' they shout with cheer,
'For aliens appeared—but we had no fear!'

With bark like armor, they jest and play,
Sharing wisdom in their own quirky way.
Branches extended for a silly slap,
'You call that a leap? Here, take a nap!'

Conversations flow as sap in spring,
Filling the woods with laughter and zing.
Every tree's a expert in humor divine,
Come join the chat, it's simply sublime!

The Tincture of Time

Time's a potion brewed with flair,
In forests where giants share a stare.
Every ring in their trunks reveals,
A tale so funny, you'll spin on your heels.

Tick-tock goes the clock, but who's counting?
With roots so deep, they keep recounting.
From the tiniest insect to the clouds above,
This wacky world is what they love.

Old patterns dance beneath the sun,
Prancing shadows say, 'Oh, what fun!'
They giggle together like children at play,
As if sweetness of time just melts all away.

In every whisper, a twinkle's cast,
From the past's embrace, laughter is vast.
These towering jesters, wise and spry,
Invite you to join—come, don't be shy!

Solid Sage of the Wilderness

Solid and wise, standing proud and grand,
The sage of the forest, a quirky band.
With leaves like wings, they embark on a spree,
While critters below join in jubilee.

Mighty sage with hair that's mossy and green,
Plays hide-and-seek with the dappled sheen.
'What's that noise?' they say with glee,
Oh, just a raccoon—so carefree!

Stories are spun like webs of delight,
Every branch a stage in the fading light.
Nature's comedy, splendid and true,
Woven in laughter, like morning dew.

A solid sage, with chuckles to share,
Brings harmony to all, no need to despair.
In the wild, they remind us each day,
That laughter's the language, come join the play!

Lifeblood of the Evergreen Giants

Deep in the woods where the tall ones stand,
A squirrel's got plans with a nut in his hand.
He nods to a tree with a grin oh so wide,
"Let's throw a feast, let's not just abide!"

Leaves gossip about the critters below,
While branches dance lightly in the breezy show.
"Did you hear? The owl's lost a feather,
He'll never out-dance us in this lovely weather!"

The beetles are buzzing, the ants take a stroll,
Elk's swapping stories, feeling quite bold.
"Last spring's a tale that beats all the rest,
Why I nearly danced right off of my nest!"

So here in the grove where the laughter won't cease,
Nature's a circus, in joy and in peace.
Under the shadows of giants so tall,
Life's a big joke, with a punchline for all!

In the Shade of Whispering Sisters

Two trees stand tall, they share every tale,
One saying, "Did you see that deer? Quite pale!"
"Oh yes!" said the other, with leaves all aflutter,
"Last week, it slipped on an old slice of butter!"

The fungi below giggle, a cheeky crew,
Their jokes as they sprout, all random and new.
A raccoon rolls by, wearing a mask of delight,
"Have you heard? The owl's got a late-night fright!"

Variables of nature don't take a long pause,
When beetles debate the best way to cause
A ruckus in mulchy, where smells create height,
Every whispering sister gleams under moonlight.

So let us all join in this merry charade,
For every old tree has a voice, a crusade.
In the shade of these sisters, where secrets unfold,
Each giggle and whisper is worth more than gold!

Trails of Time in the Timber

Winding through woods that hold laughs in their core,
A family of squirrels keeps tally of lore.
"I saw you yesterday, with that acorn so fat!"
"Hey, I might have dropped it, but who's counting that?"

Beneath every branch, a new story arises,
Old turtles debate who the fastest one fries.
They take little bets trailing back to the stream,
"I'd win in the end, just watch me, I beam!"

The shadows do stretch as day turns to night,
And the chirps of the crickets bring pure delight.
"Have you tried jumping over that twig on the trail?"
Easy as pie, till you slip and then wail!

So tread with a chuckle through trails lined in grace,
With laughter resounding, we all find our place.
In the timber so grand, with our fibrous peers,
Every step brings a giggle to calm all your fears.

The Hymn of the High Canopy

Up in the heights where the breezes conspire,
The avian chorus lifts mood to aspire.
"Sing loud!" croaks a crow, "Add a twist and a turn!"
While the woodpecker joins in, it's his time to churn!

Lush leaves sway gently, they jig and they jive,
"Who's got the best dance?" They sing and they thrive.
Chatters of monkeys mix in with delight,
"Last night's moon was a hoot; what a wondrous sight!"

The breeze tickles branches, plays tricks with the remnant,

Gives all who listen their own bit of element.
"Catch that funny hat from the wind if you can!"
A hundred laughs rise, nature's elaborate plan!

So raise up your voices in this grand old sky,
With merriment high, let your spirits fly.
For in this vast canopy, we dance as we please,
Even the tallest tree giggles in the breeze!

Tides of Time Beneath Bark

Tall trees laugh at the passing years,
With roots that tickle the earth's old fears.
Branches sway, a giggle in the breeze,
They share tales that bring you to your knees.

Foliage hides not just birds, but a jest,
Fungi join in for a fun little quest.
Squirrels dance to the rhythm of age,
While whispering secrets, to turn a new page.

Each ring tells a story of rainy days,
Of sunlight's embrace and mischievous ways.
Laughter echoes through the forest wide,
Where time bends and twists, like the branches they ride

So when you wander 'neath their green arrays,
Join in their fun, let your worries decay.
For the giants of wood hold a playful heart,
In each slice of their bark, you'll find nature's art.

Dreamscape of the Green Giants

In a dream where giants twirl and leap,
They trade old jokes while the owls just peep.
With laughter echoing through the sunny glade,
Each chuckle from them never seems to fade.

Bees buzz in rhythm, swaying in time,
While squirrels narrate stories in rhyme.
The leaves shimmy like a comical show,
As the shadows dance, putting on quite a glow.

A parade of critters, what a sight to behold,
With acorns and laughter, their treasures untold.
In the realm of giants, where silliness reigns,
Nature's humor flows in whimsical veins.

So tiptoe through dreams where the giants reside,
Join in the laughter, take fun in your stride.
For in this green world of whimsical cheer,
You'll find joy in nature, so simple and clear.

The Wisdom of Weathered Wood

Old trees grin with the wisdom they bear,
As bugs tell tales of a life debonair.
With knots like wrinkles, and a barky smile,
They've seen storms and sunshine, each for a while.

Woodpecker knocks, "Did you hear that one?"
As crows chime in, "Hoo boy, let's have fun!"
The stories they share make the sun feel bright,
While critters below offer comic delight.

Moss grows soft on the tales that are told,
While a laughing brook sparkles with old gold.
Each loop of their bark holds a joke or a pun,
Time is just laughter, when the day is done.

So listen closely to the trees' wise grins,
For they know the joy where true life begins.
Let their chuckles lighten your heart that it's good,
To revel in nature, as only wood could.

Harmony of the Woodland Whispers

In whispers of trees, you'll find laughter's tune,
As leaves share quips with the squirrels and raccoons.
A gentle breeze carries witty remarks,
While shadows dance cheerfully, leaving their marks.

The crickets chirp jokes in a night-time spree,
While starlit skies giggle, "Can you see me?"
Every rustling branch holds a playful rhyme,
Echoing joy in the heart of the time.

Underneath the boughs, secrets slide and twist,
Making a tapestry, where no fun is missed.
The gathering critters revel in delight,
Turning the forest into a playful sight.

So next time you wander where the tall trees grow,
Join in their whispers, let your spirit flow.
In the harmony found in woodland cheer,
The joys of nature are crystal clear.

Nature's Cryptic Correspondence

In the grove where trees play chess,
The squirrels plot with acorn finesse.
'Hey, did you see that birdie strut?'
'No, I missed it, got stuck in a rut!'

Leaves whisper tales of who's got swag,
One branch declares, 'I've got a whole rag!'
The roots giggle, 'Did you find that nut?'
While branches wave, giving trees a shut-up!

Moss giggles softly, 'I've got the scoop,'
While mushrooms dance in a mushroom troop.
And just when you think it's all just play,
A pinecone shushes, 'No work today!'

So come and join this prankster crew,
Where nature's humor is never through.
In every ring, in every tick,
There's laughter hidden—find it quick!

The Twilight of the Timberland

Under the canopy, the owls hoot loud,
'What's the scoop?' they crow to the crowd.
A raccoon stumbles, wearing three hats,
'Thought I was clever, just look at that!'

Trees gossip in their wooden tones,
'Who's stealing nuts? That rascal, Jones!'
A fox appears, all sly with glee,
'Those nuts? They were left here for me!'

A deer prances in, quite a sight,
'Is it twilight, or just my fright?'
The shadows chuckle, shadows collide,
'Oh dear, don't worry, it's just your pride!'

As fireflies flicker, playing their tricks,
The moon rolls its eyes, 'What a mix!'
In this wood, where the oddballs dwell,
Every twist is a tale to tell!

Tales that Rise with the Mist

In the morning fog, stories float and swirl,
A chipmunk winks, 'Got the latest whirl!'
'What's up with the old crow?' asks a lark,
'He's picking fights with the post at the park!'

Mist wraps around, like a soft, cozy coat,
'The early owl thinks he's quite the gloat.'
'What's he got that we don't?' chimes a hare,
'Well, wisdom and fluff, if you really care.'

Among the ferns, a beetle blinks,
'Life's a joke, don't you think?'
So they gather, a merry little crew,
With laughter echoing as the fog bids adieu!

The sun breaks through, a shimmery beam,
Each creature chirps, 'Let's chase our dream!'
In every rustle and sigh you find,
A tale of mischief, joy intertwined!

A Locket of Leaves and Lore

In the heart of the woods, where the cool breeze flows,
A squirrel twirls, flaunting his new clothes.
'Chairman of the Nutty Club,' he claims,
While pine cones whisper all of his names!

Branches creak with playful delight,
Sharing old puns while taking flight.
A laughing woodpecker taps a soft beat,
'Like a drumline, but cuter—can't be beat!'

Twigs clink together, forming a band,
While leaves do the cha-cha, oh so grand!
'The wind is our DJ,' the branches agree,
'Let's dance in a conga, wild and free!'

As stars wink down, joining the spree,
Nature holds a locket—a secret, you see.
In every giggle, every rustling cheer,
A hidden charm for all who come near!

Cradled in Time's Embrace

Once there lived a tree so tall,
It chuckled at the squirrels' brawl.
A party hat that fit just right,
It danced beneath the moonlit night.

The sun would tickle its bark,
While chipmunks played a pyramidal lark.
With roots so deep, it knew the score,
'You think you're wise? I've seen much more!'

The winds would whisper, 'Hey, old chap!'
With leaves like hats, a leafy cap.
It spun tall tales of years gone by,
While birds looked on with a knowing sigh.

So if you venture through the glade,
Listen close, lend an ear, be not afraid.
You'll hear the laughter of trees so grand,
They've got wild stories, all unplanned.

Spirit of the Old Growth

In a grove where giggles sprout,
The old trees tease, 'What's life about?'
Branching out, they share their tricks,
With wise old wisdom, humor mixed.

One claimed to know the best potato,
A root so big, it set a new rate-o!
The birds would chirp and squeak with glee,
'This tree's pathetic, can't even see!'

A beaver grinned, with a toothy smile,
'I'll gnaw your tales, just give me a while!'
And so they laughed, in sunny patches,
As sunlight spilled in golden batches.

With knots and gnarls, a jolly sight,
They sauntered through the starry night.
Their laughter echoed in every grove,
In this old hideaway, their stories wove.

Echoing Silence of the Woodlands

In silence sat a towering chap,
Wearing a mossy, greenish cap.
The groundlings whispered tales of fame,
'This tree's a legend, it's got no shame!'

Between the limbs, a gossip flew,
'Have you heard what the owls do?'
They party like they're on a spree,
While raccoons steal the tree's own key!

A rustle here, a chuckle there,
The wise old trunk just hugs the air.
'You think you know? I've seen it all,
From ants to elk, I answer the call!'

With laughter stitched in every ring,
A silent tree can still be king.
So stroll the path, and laugh out loud,
For nature's trees are always proud!

Crescendo of the Evergreen

At dawn, the trees would wake and stretch,
With branches swaying, all the bets.
'Who can stand still, don't make a peep!'
While owls giggle, trying not to sleep.

A sprightly sapling shared a joke,
'Why did the pine stand by the oak?'
To show it off, with roots so wide,
While laughter flowed on nature's tide.

The breeze would tease, 'Oh, what a zest!
Bigger's better, come be my guest!'
With acorns bouncing, and petals to sway,
Life's a laugh when you're made of clay.

So, join the trees in their playful sound,
Where echoes of joy can always be found.
In nature's jest, let your worries retreat,
For every leaf holds a giggle, sweet!

www.ingramcontent.com/pod-product-compliance
Lightning Source LLC
Chambersburg PA
CBHW051639160426
43209CB00004B/720